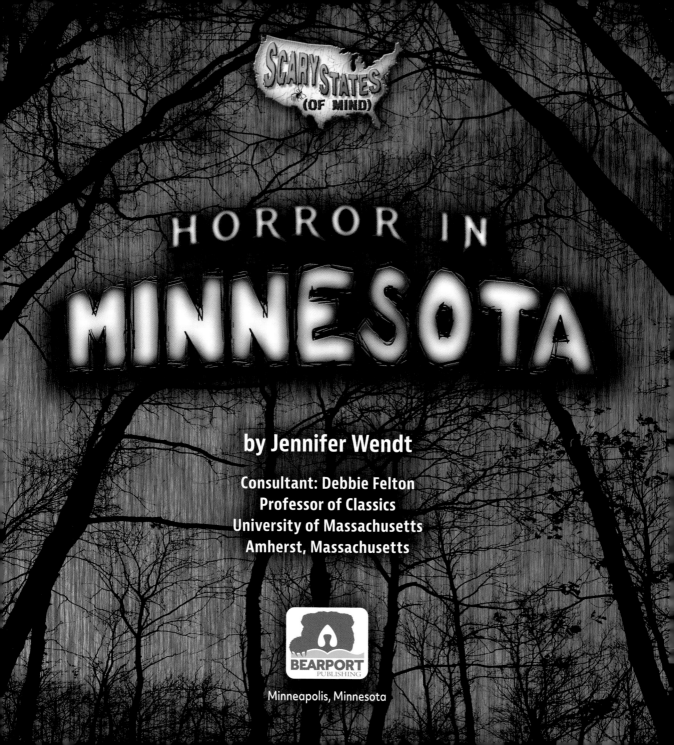

SCARY STATES
(OF MIND)

HORROR IN
MINNESOTA

by Jennifer Wendt

Consultant: Debbie Felton
Professor of Classics
University of Massachusetts
Amherst, Massachusetts

BEARPORT
PUBLISHING

Minneapolis, Minnesota

Credits

Cover, © Kim Jones, © Joe Ferrer/Shutterstock, © Robyn Mackenzie/Shutterstock, and © Monika Surzin/Shutterstock; 3, John Brueske; 4-5, , © Kim Jones, © MarynaG/Shutterstock, © LTim/Shutterstock, © Holly Kuchera/Shutterstock, © AB Photographie/Shutterstock, and © UfaBizPhoto/Shutterstock; 6, © Alan Smillie/Shutterstock; 7, © Dornseif-Photography/Shutterstock; 7b, © Christian Darkin/Shutterstock; 8, © Scinauticando/Wikimedia Commons/Creative Commons; 9, © Khadi Ganiev/Shutterstock; 11, © Akanee konthon/Shutterstock; 12, © adike/Shutterstock; 13, © Joe Gough/Shutterstock; 14, © patrimonio designs ltd/Shutterstock; 15, © MarenHandrich/Shutterstock; 17, © LeManna/Shutterstock and © andryuha1981/Shutterstock; 18, © Khakimullin Aleksandr/Shutterstock; 19, © McGhiever/Wikimedia Commons/Creative Commons; 20, © fluke samed/Shutterstock; 21, © Rocksweeper/Shutterstock and © elbud/Shutterstock; 23, © Craig Hinton/Shutterstock; and 24, © Fer Gregory/Shutterstock.

President: Jen Jenson
Director of Product Development: Spencer Brinker
Editor: Allison Juda
Designer: Micah Edel
Cover: Kim Jones

Library of Congress Cataloging-in-Publication Data

Names: Wendt, Jennifer, author.
Title: Horror in Minnesota / Jennifer Wendt.
Description: Minneapolis, Minnesota : Bearport Publishing Company, 2020. | Series: Scary states (of mind) | Includes bibliographical references and index.
Identifiers: LCCN 2020008723 (print) | LCCN 2020008724 (ebook) | ISBN 9781647470760 (library binding) | ISBN 9781647470869 (ebook)
Subjects: LCSH: Haunted places—Minnesota—Juvenile literature. | Minnesota—Miscellanea—Juvenile literature.
Classification: LCC BF1472.U6 W46 2020 (print) | LCC BF1472.U6 (ebook) | DDC 133.109776—dc23
LC record available at https://lccn.loc.gov/2020008723
LC ebook record available at https://lccn.loc.gov/2020008724

For more information, write to Bearport Publishing, 5357 Penn Avenue South, Minneapolis, MN 55419. Printed in the United States of America.

CONTENTS

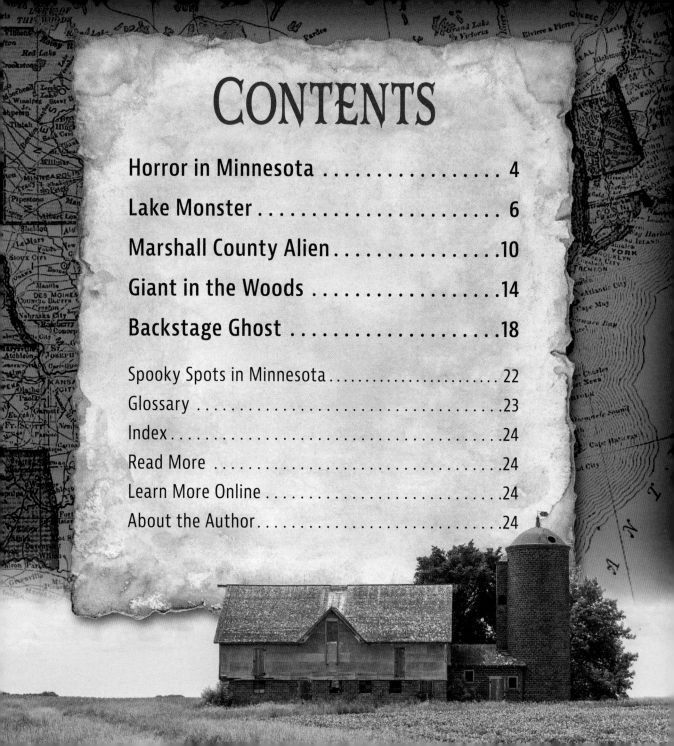

HORROR IN MINNESOTA

Minnesota has beautiful lakes, the mighty Mississippi River, and forests that are hundreds of years old. But did you know there is a spooky side to this lovely state? Watch out for monsters and ghosts hidden in its lakes, forests, and dark skies!

Get ready to read four spooky stories about Minnesota. Turn the page . . . if you dare.

LAKE MONSTER

Lake Pepin, Lake City

Is there a mystery swimming in Lake Pepin's depths? In the late 1600s, a French explorer wrote about a serpent that was at least 8 feet (2.4 m) long gliding through the waters of Lake Pepin. The Dakota people from the area also have stories of a lake monster. They used large, strong canoes to protect themselves against a creature big enough to **capsize** a smaller boat.

Lake Pepin

Area residents named this shy lake monster Pepie. Lake City **lore** even claims that Pepie is partly responsible for another reason the lake is famous. On a bright, moonlit night in 1922, Ralph Samuelson saw Pepie gliding across Lake Pepin. He was **inspired** by the sight and soon invented the sport of water skiing.

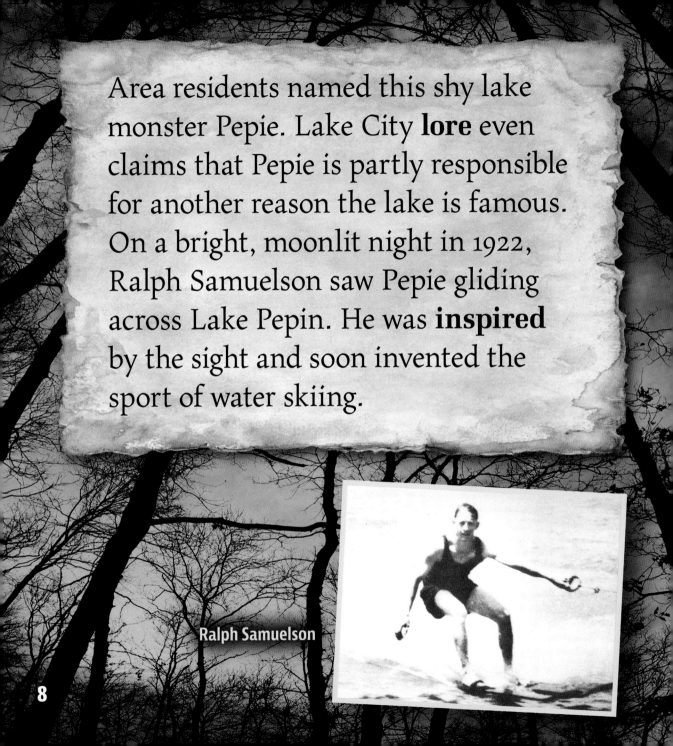

Ralph Samuelson

An illustration of the Loch Ness Monster

Lake Pepin is a lot like Scotland's Loch Ness. Are Pepie and the famous Loch Ness Monster the same kind of creature?

Marshall County Alien

Warren, Marshall County

In August 1979, Officer Val Johnson was driving along a country road near the city of Warren when he saw something strange in the sky. There was a light hovering about 3 ft (0.9 m) off the ground. He drove toward it. Suddenly, the object went at him. Half an hour later, he woke up in his damaged car. His face and eyes were burned, and a lump was forming on his head.

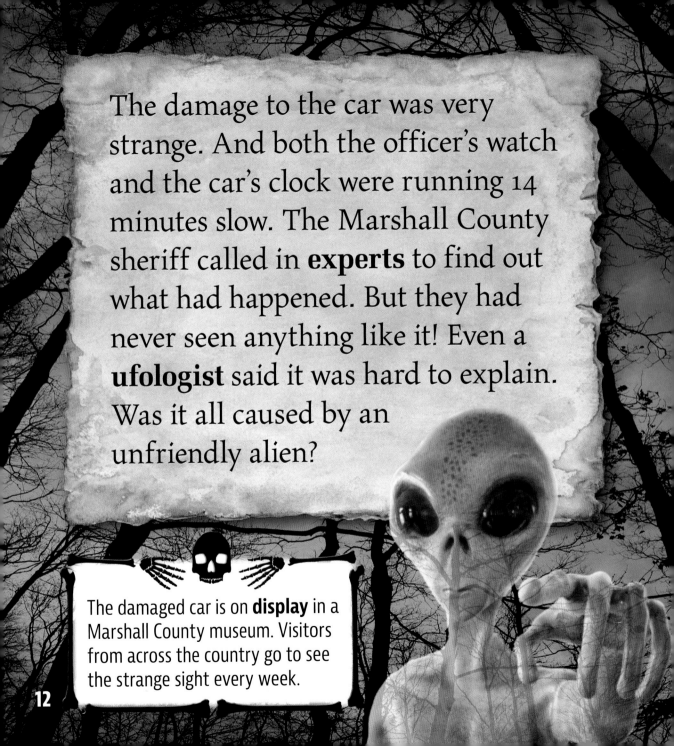

The damage to the car was very strange. And both the officer's watch and the car's clock were running 14 minutes slow. The Marshall County sheriff called in **experts** to find out what had happened. But they had never seen anything like it! Even a **ufologist** said it was hard to explain. Was it all caused by an unfriendly alien?

The damaged car is on **display** in a Marshall County museum. Visitors from across the country go to see the strange sight every week.

Giant In The Woods

Roseau County

Is a giant with glowing eyes, long fangs, and sharp claws roaming the woods in Roseau County? Some people seem to think so!

There have been sightings of the Wendigo giant since the late 1800s. Each report was followed by a sudden death.

The Wendigo is said to be good at hiding and hunting. Some think it can control the weather.

15

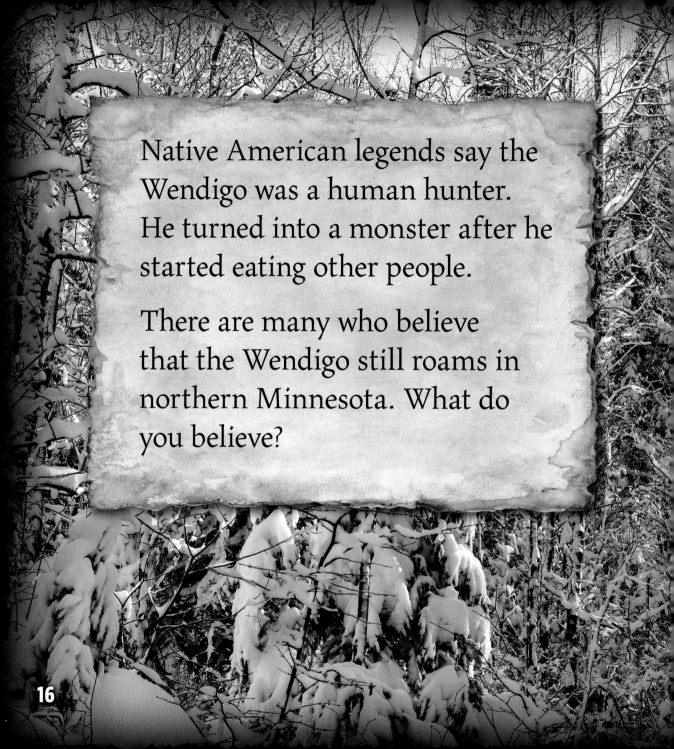

Native American legends say the Wendigo was a human hunter. He turned into a monster after he started eating other people.

There are many who believe that the Wendigo still roams in northern Minnesota. What do you believe?

Backstage Ghost

Fitzgerald Theater, St. Paul

Although it was built in 1910, the Fitzgerald Theater's haunting history has been more recent. In 1985, an old note was discovered during building **renovations**. It was written to a man named Ben who worked in the theater long ago. Soon after, people started seeing Ben's ghost wandering the halls. Workers' tools disappeared and empty bottles of wine were found in the theater. Were they left behind by Ben the ghost?

To Ben

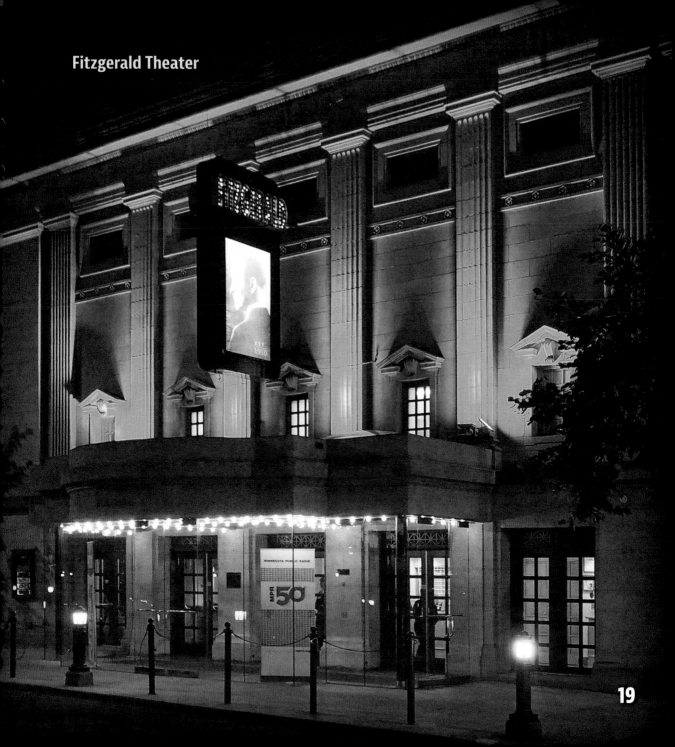

Fitzgerald Theater

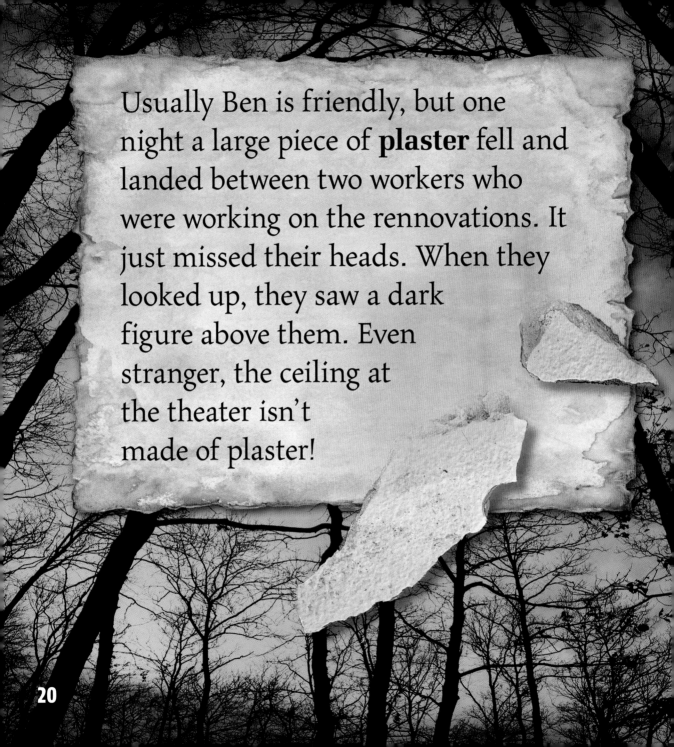

Usually Ben is friendly, but one night a large piece of **plaster** fell and landed between two workers who were working on the rennovations. It just missed their heads. When they looked up, they saw a dark figure above them. Even stranger, the ceiling at the theater isn't made of plaster!

SPOOKY SPOTS IN MINNESOTA

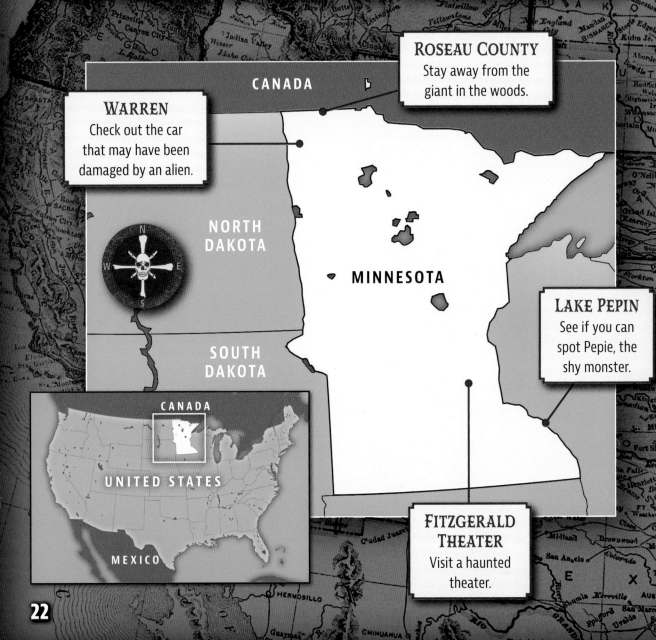

ROSEAU COUNTY
Stay away from the giant in the woods.

WARREN
Check out the car that may have been damaged by an alien.

CANADA

NORTH DAKOTA

MINNESOTA

SOUTH DAKOTA

LAKE PEPIN
See if you can spot Pepie, the shy monster.

CANADA

UNITED STATES

MEXICO

FITZGERALD THEATER
Visit a haunted theater.

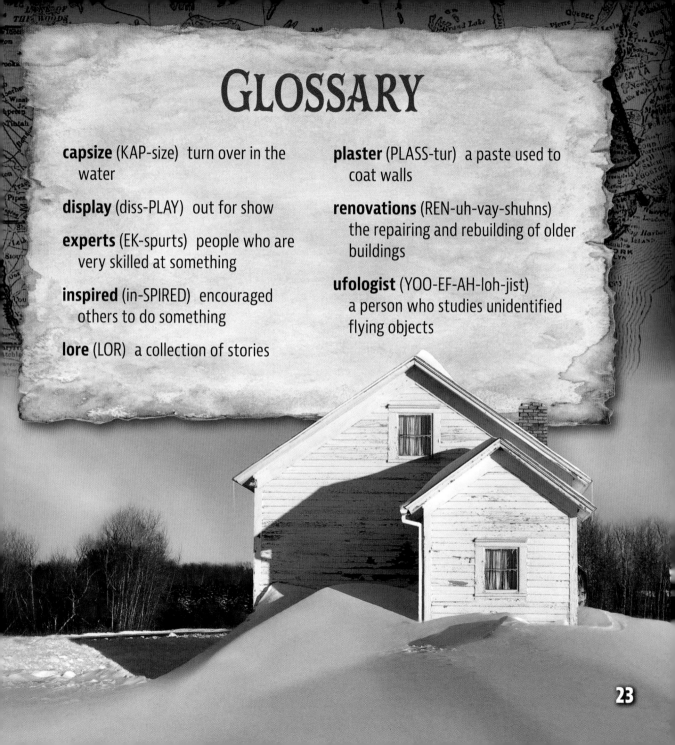

GLOSSARY

capsize (KAP-size) turn over in the water

display (diss-PLAY) out for show

experts (EK-spurts) people who are very skilled at something

inspired (in-SPIRED) encouraged others to do something

lore (LOR) a collection of stories

plaster (PLASS-tur) a paste used to coat walls

renovations (REN-uh-vay-shuhns) the repairing and rebuilding of older buildings

ufologist (YOO-EF-AH-loh-jist) a person who studies unidentified flying objects

INDEX

Read More

Camisa, Kathryn. *Ghostly Theaters (Tiptoe into Scary Places).* New York: Bearport (2018).

Rudolph, Jessica. *Alien Landing Sites (Tiptoe into Scary Places).* New York: Bearport (2018).

Learn More Online

1. Go to **www.factsurfer.com**
2. Enter "**Horror in Minnesota**" into the search box.
3. Click on the cover of this book to see a list of websites.

About the Author

Jennifer Wendt lives in Minnesota. She grew up on a farm where there were always spooky sounds. She used to visit a graveyard in a nearby field to try and catch snakes.